# Pacifics on the
# SOUTH WESTERN

**Tony Molyneaux &
Kevin Robertson**

Ian Allan
PUBLISHING

*Front cover:* Rebuilt 'West Country' No 34024 *Tamar Valley* passes through Eastleigh station at the head of a down Weymouth working. Notice the customary luggage van leading. Although surviving until the end of steam, this locomotive was recalled by Eastleigh men who worked on her as being one of the rougher engines on which to ride.

*Back cover:* From ground level the impact of a Pacific running at speed was impressive, the effect being accentuated when the running lines were raised due to the ballast. Such was the case just north of Allbrook, where Tony's camera has caught 'West Country' No 34006 *Bude* heading north on the up through line with a Waterloo-bound passenger working in May 1963. As is well known Bulleid's original design caused smoke and steam to hang around the area of the casing, thus restricting the already limited view ahead. *Bude* was one of the class selected for experimentation in an attempt to remedy this problem and was fitted with extended smoke-deflectors, which it carried right to the end. They certainly appear to be working here!

*Title page:* Pacific in full flight. Rebuilt 'West Country' No 34095 *Brentor* passes Hinton Admiral station ('for Highcliffe on Sea') on 23 April 1962. The locomotive was not yet in its final form, as the following year it would be further modified with an anti-glare screen, spark-arrester and alterations to the pipework of the mechanical lubricators. It would also receive no fewer than four further light or casual repairs and was destined to be one of the final steam engines at work on the Southern Region, until July 1967. Neglected perhaps in its final years by its owners, No 34095 was always regarded as a 'goodun'.

*Above right:* 'West Country' No 34099 *Lynmouth* in charge of the up 'Atlantic Coast Express' at Sidmouth Junction at mid-day on 12 July 1960. The route at this point has been downhill for the past five miles, and the fireman looks to be enjoying a breather — as well he might, for shortly the line will reach its lowest point, after which it will be uphill again for the climb through Honiton Tunnel towards Seaton Junction and the next stop, at Axminster.

*Right:* In the opinion of many (including the photographer and the author) the rebuilt Bulleid Pacific type was, aesthetically at least, far superior to the original design. There were those who felt they were perhaps too similar to the Standard Pacific designs, but as both appeared in the same decade this is perhaps not entirely surprising. Bathed in evening sunlight on 11 September 1965, rebuilt 'Battle of Britain' No 34071 *601 Squadron* reposes outside Eastleigh shed, its clean(ish) livery in stark contrast to the filthy 'Standard' just visible in the background.

# Introduction

It is always a pleasure to be asked to compile a new book, and this is no exception. Indeed, in many respects it is also rather special; special because, yet again, it has been a pleasure as well as a privilege to have access to Tony Molyneaux's archive of unpublished material but also, on a personal note, because I can add the odd snippet of information (gleaned from talking to Southern crews) on particular locomotives, which fact will, I hope, make this more than merely a collection of new photographs.

I must confess to a certain affinity to the Bulleid breed — not, I should add, from any personal experience in working on them, either in revenue-earning service or in preservation, but simply because, in my childhood, they were the first engines I clearly recall seeing, and the impression they then made on a youngster has never totally faded. Speak to others with like-minded railway interest and they too will often admit that it was also their first impressions of railways that have created the most lasting impressions. Accordingly those who cherish the work of Collett, Stanier and Gresley will have their own particular favourites, although I hope like me will also admit in the end that we just 'like steam trains'.

In a book of this kind it would be foolhardy to suggest that its appeal will be as great in all the far-flung corners of England, Wales and Scotland as it will be (hopefully) in the South. But prepare to be amazed, for I have

First published 2006

ISBN (10) 0 7110 3129 0
ISBN (13) 978 0 7110 3129 6

© Ian Allan Publishing 2006

Published by Ian Allan Publishing

an imprint of Ian Allan Publishing Ltd, Hersham, Surrey KT12 4RG
Printed in England by Ian Allan Printing Ltd, Hersham, Surrey KT12 4RG

0602/B

Visit the Ian Allan Publishing website at www.ianallanpublishing.com

legitimately included a few Pacifics of other than the Bulleid breed, which were recorded by Tony's camera on workings into the South Western area.

Regrettably my own recollections of the Bulleid type tend to be of grimy locomotives leaking steam from almost every joint, although those that were fresh from works or had recently received the attention of the cleaner's cloth displayed a welcome freshness. For this selection I have, with Tony's consent, generally selected photographs depicting locomotives in relatively clean condition — not necessarily ex works but typical, I hope, of the years from c1956 to 1967, without any definite emphasis on a particular theme. Consciously also there is no section dealing with withdrawn engines. But as the pace of withdrawal quickened through to July 1967 so the ranks of withdrawn engines grew at places such as Nine Elms, Basingstoke, Eastleigh, Salisbury and Weymouth, presenting a melancholy sight to railwayman and traveller alike.

I well recall travelling on a daily basis behind steam to school from the early 1960s onwards. The choice available to me was in fact a predictable DEMU or an often late-running steam-hauled service emanating from what was by now the Western Region. As far as I was concerned there was no contest, even if my delayed arrival sometimes resulted in a sprint up the school hill and some red-faced embarrassment in front of the teachers. I think my contemporaries regarded such activity with a kind of resigned amusement, but 40 years later it is I who can have the last laugh, having been able to turn a hobby into a full-time occupation and thus indulge a continuing passion for the railways of yesteryear.

Witnessing the Bulleid breed at work on the Southern Region was vastly different from seeing such locomotives today on the various preserved lines, where, fortunately, a number still survive. Starting a train of anything up to 12 coaches — plus, perhaps, a van or two — could result in a violent wheelslip; indeed most times it seemed to. As an observer I was disappointed when it didn't, unable at the time to appreciate the skill of the driver in controlling what was a somewhat difficult machine to start. None of this, of course, was assisted by the obvious fact that these very starting points were used also by countless other engines, each of which in turn had no doubt contributed to the various deposits of oil and grease that could have such a profound effect on more than 100 tons of machinery. This aspect of starting a heavy train is another area where the appearance of the railway itself has changed. Enthusiasts will lament the passing of steam, mechanical signalling, loose-coupled freight trains and the like, but also gone are the associated trademarks of each — water columns, grease and oil between the rails at the end of every platform.

In sound and sight the Bulleid breed displayed a difference too compared with the products of Maunsell and Riddles, the two designers responsible for most other steam designs seen in the same period. A Bulleid Pacific, with its three-cylinder design, rarely produced a regular exhaust beat, instead having an almost 'dot-pause-double dot-pause' trademark when getting away — something, I have learned, they shared with a number of the Gresley types to be found at places like King's Cross. Of course some engines were worse affected than others, and as wear occurred so the unbalanced exhaust became more noticeable when starting, although as the cut-off lengthened and speed progressed so this sound would itself disappear, giving way to the second feature of the design whereby the exhaust steam would fail to dissipate completely, leaving a cloud around the front of the smokebox (of the rebuilt locomotives) or alongside the air smoothed casing (of the un-rebuilt engines).

I must say that pure ignorance on my part meant that in the case of the rebuilt engines I honestly thought for a while that this was the result of steam escaping from the top of the smokebox door — until one day a kindly driver at Eastleigh put me straight. This was the start of a number of visits to Eastleigh shed, where for some time it was possible to walk around without interruption, often discovering for oneself which parts of an engine were likely to be hot and/or particularly dirty. Sadly permission for such forays was less likely to be granted as 1967 approached, the activities of a few

*Above right:* Having set the scene with the views of the Light Pacifics in original and modified form, let us now turn to the 'Merchant Navy' class and one of Tony's early views recording No 35024 *East Asiatic Company* at Salisbury with the London-bound 'Atlantic Coast Express' on 3 August 1956. This locomotive was then less than eight years old, being one of the final 10 of the class built, in 1948/9. Destined to be rebuilt in April 1959, it would be withdrawn less than six years later, in January 1965, having already been relegated from front-line duties as being due a heavy overhaul. This it would not receive, on account of the BRB edict prohibiting such work on steam, and instead No 35024 was to languish at Eastleigh shed, devoid of nameplates and coupling rods, until towed away to South Wales in April 1965, being reduced to scrap the following month.

*Right:* First of the 'Merchant Navy' locomotives to be rebuilt was No 35018 *British India Line*, which appeared in its new guise in February 1956 and is seen here at Eastleigh in August 1959. According to E. S. Beavor, in his book *Steam was my Calling* (Ian Allan, 1974), the new inside cylinder castings necessary for the rebuilt engines had to be produced outside the UK, although whether this applied to all the rebuilds or just some is not certain. The pipework on this locomotive differed very slightly from that on subsequent rebuilds.

irresponsible visitors and trespassers affecting the pleasure of the majority. However, before this happened I was able to speak to (and, fortunately, document the views of) several of the crews on the subject of particular engines. For what purpose I did this — and equally why I deemed it necessary down the years to retain my jottings — I cannot recall, but I am very glad I did, for here at last is the ideal opportunity to present the opinions of some of those drivers, firemen and fitters. It is a matter of regret that I did not record the names of most of those involved, instead being intent on noting the views and preferences of the men for one machine over another.

The general consensus among footplate crews was that the Bulleid type was preferable for fast running, although it seems the rebuilt engines always had to be worked slightly harder in their new form. A 'Standard' was also considered fast but was disliked because of cab draughts, although conversely the enclosed cab of the Bulleid Pacific was an unpleasant place to be on a hot summer's day. The fitters and foremen held a different perspective, several expressing a wish for the designer to witness their difficulties in gaining access to the oil bath and the like on the original engines; the foreman, meanwhile, having allocated a particular engine to a job, would almost hold his breath to ascertain whether it would complete the booked diagram without suffering a defect of one sort or another. In this respect the 'Standard' and Maunsell-designed engines were both easier to work on and more predictable, although all admitted that a Bulleid on a good day was probably without equal.

From the previous paragraph it might appear as if the Bulleid Pacifics were bad engines, but far from it: they were as good (or bad) as any other running in the latter days of steam in Britain, and it is personal preference that will win the day. Sadly, of course, it is no longer possible, other than on those rare occasions when a main-line special is run, to witness a Pacific in full flight from Waterloo *en route* for Exeter or Bournemouth. Perhaps this is the one area where heritage operations cannot recapture the spirit of days gone by.

Purely as a pipe-dream — or if I were ever to win the jackpot on the lottery — it would be lovely to recapture the sight and sound of, say, the up 'Royal Wessex' and so witness the amazement in the eyes of the 21st-century morning commuter at Southampton or Winchester as, following the announcement of the imminent arrival of the Waterloo train, a Pacific and 10 green coaches turned up. To us schoolboys this particular morning service also had a nickname (in reality equally applicable to any number of the morning services) — 'the Egg and Bacon' — on account of the aroma which lingered after its passing.

By now the reader will clearly have gathered that in this particular introduction there has been no attempt to regurgitate a potted history of the Bulleid engines themselves. Save for reminiscences there is probably little else new now left to recollect, although for the sake of completeness some individual engine history is included in the captions where appropriate. But there are two details applicable to the operation of Pacifics on the South Western that may not be so well known. The first is that, had events transpired as intended, this book might also have legitimately included within its pages views of the Stanier 'Duchess' class, for there was a serious proposal to transfer a number of these to the Southern Region *c*1964 following their displacement by electrification from Euston. Sadly restricted clearances — particularly, it was stated, at Battledown, near Basingstoke — put paid to this. At an unknown date there was also a proposal to utilise a Bulleid 'Merchant Navy' boiler on the frames of a 'Britannia', the rationale being that the simplicity of the 'Britannia' frames and motion allied to the extraordinary steam-raising capabilities of the 'Merchant Navy' boiler would have made for a remarkable engine. This was evidently vetoed on the grounds of weight, although the obvious solution would surely have been to use a 'West Country' boiler, which was both shorter and slimmer and consequently lighter. Perhaps some preservationist might today consider resurrecting the idea; it would make for a very interesting result!

We are now fast approaching the 40th anniversary of the end of steam on the South Western, the last bastion having been the main line from Waterloo to Bournemouth and Weymouth, although (as recounted above) included within these pages are many earlier views. Unfortunately it is simply not possible to squeeze illustrations of all 140 Southern Pacifics into an 80-page book, so my apologies if a particular favourite engine is not featured.

As time passes, so those who remember steam in everyday service grow older, and memories fade. Although still resident in Hampshire I no longer live within earshot of the Bournemouth main line, where on numerous occasions it was possible to lie in bed and hear, instead of vehicular traffic, the sound of a Bulleid with its uneven beat working its way up the long climb between Eastleigh and Roundwood Summit. Thankyou, then, Mr Bulleid, for affording such memories, and thankyou, Tony Molyneaux, for recording them and allowing them to be shared. As ever it has been a pleasure and a privilege working with both of you.

*Kevin Robertson*
Southampton
November 2005

No 34003 *Plymouth* in Eastleigh Works on 24 October 1959 — yet
according to official records it was not there at the time! Rebuilt two years
previously, it was to be one of the earlier casualties among such locomotives,
being withdrawn in September 1964.

*Above:* Contrasting from No 35018 on page 5, here is No 35028 *Clan Line* right at the very end of her operational days. The locomotive is in full flight on the down through line just south of Shawford at the head of one of the BR-sponsored 'Farewell to Steam' workings from Waterloo to Weymouth on Saturday 2 July 1967. Nameplates have been restored for the occasion, although the smokebox number-plate is missing.

*Right:* Unusually Tony's records fail to identify this 'Merchant Navy', seen heading a school special northbound through Eastleigh on 28 April 1961. However, 40-plus years on, it can be revealed that it is No 35027 *Port Line* hauling what purports to be Bulleid coach set No 237 but within which has been marshalled a BR Mk 1 buffet car.

No 35019 *French Line CGT* at speed just west of Brockenhurst with the 10.30am Waterloo–Bournemouth on 14 October 1961. The time would be around 12.13pm, assuming the train is on schedule, this being one of the fast (two-hour) services between the two termini, with a single five-minute stop at Southampton Central. Interestingly the maximum load for this particular service was set at 400 tons.

Pride of place among the passenger services on the South Western division had to go to the 'Bournemouth Belle', of which the down working is seen here near Hinton Admiral on 23 April 1962 with No 35014 *Nederland Line* at its head.

The train consists of the then standard 12-coach formation, including some heavy 12-wheel vehicles. This was probably the heaviest regular passenger train operating in and out of Waterloo at the time.

*Left:* Two years later and the grime is starting to show. On 16 May 1964 No 35024 *East Asiatic Company* heads the up service just north of Winchester Junction, almost two thirds of the way up the long 1-in-250 gradient from Eastleigh to Litchfield Summit. By this time also the Pullman Brake Seconds at each end of the rake were occassionally replaced by standard luggage vans in chocolate and cream. The story goes that a lack of luggage space in the existing formation was resolved purely by chance when a senior member of the Pullman staff happened to see a Western Region-liveried luggage van at Clapham Junction; two were swiftly purloined for use in the 'Belle'. Once the Brake Seconds were withdrawn the formation remained basically unaltered until July 1967.

*Above:* The same working, but in the opposite direction and on a different occasion. Seemingly with a full head of steam, No 35029 *Ellerman Lines* waits at Southampton Central with the down 'Belle' on 22 August 1964. No 35029 now reposes in cut-away form at the National Railway Museum, York, having been sectioned to give visitors an inside view of the workings of a steam locomotive.

*Above:* Having depicted the grime of the final years, let us now return to 'cleaner' times with No 35021 *New Zealand Line*, seen here at Hinton Admiral on 23 April 1962 with the 12.40 Bournemouth–Waterloo, again calling only at Southampton. This was another service on which the load was restricted to 400 tons, and arrived at Bournemouth Central in two portions — one from Weymouth, the other from Bournemouth West — which were then amalgamated to form the service seen here. The engine was now a year on from its previous light intermediate overhaul and was destined to receive another of similar type at the end of the 1962 summer season.

*Above right:* Another of the final seven of the class to survive until the end of SR steam was No 35008 *Orient Line*, recorded near Allbrook (Eastleigh) in May 1961 and unusually somewhat grimy for the year. The train is the down 'Royal Wessex', which, with its numerous stops, heavy loading yet fast schedule, was in many respects more demanding on locomotives and crews than the heavier 'Bournemouth Belle'.

*Right:* The nameplate from the first of the 'Merchant Navy' class, No 35001, attached to the boiler side of the rebuilt locomotive at Eastleigh on 3 March 1963. At the time No 35001 had only recently emerged from the neighbouring works after overhaul and so was based at the shed for the purpose of running in. Either side of the nameplate are the tubes and covers for the sandboxes.

*Far right:* Another nameplate, this time from No 35022, the bright brasswork contrasting sharply with the work-stained paintwork of the boiler. The plates themselves were cast and fitted in three sections, the main piece being the circular centre portion. By this time (6 June 1964) the locomotive had just over six months left in service, being withdrawn in January 1965 simply because the necessary repairs could not be authorised.

*Left:* Another grimy engine, this time No 35010 *Blue Star*, leaves Platform 1 at Southampton Central with a Waterloo working on 4 March 1959. For the period the external condition is nothing short of a disgrace, which is surprising when one bears in mind that this was then an Exmouth Junction engine; possibly Nine Elms had 'borrowed' it upon arrival for a round-trip. Four months later the locomotive was admitted to works for attention.

*Above:* An interesting view recorded on 17 July 1965 from the public footbridge across the main lines at Millbrook, showing well the 'dog-leg' in the down fast line at this point. To the left are the Millbrook yards, at the time seemingly dominated by cement wagons but today part of the Southampton Freightliner complex. The train is the 3.35pm from Waterloo to Bournemouth West, which included a number of intermediate stops in its 2¼ hour schedule. In charge is No 35007, which, with sister engine No 35028, had been one of the last two of the class to receive a heavy general repair, in 1964. No 35007 was renowned as a 'flyer' and is known to have reached 98mph just three days before the end of steam, although by then the ride was probably a bit rough at such speeds!

*Above:* Steam to spare as No 35028 *Clan Line*, passes the north end of the
Eastleigh yards with the 4.30pm ex Waterloo on 17 August 1966. Another
multi-stop service, this was destined for Weymouth. The presence of grey
smoke, indicative of recent firing, and the fact that the engine is blowing off
steam suggest that the train has just encountered an unexpected signal check at
this point. The first 'Merchant Navy' to be preserved, having been purchased
direct from BR in 1967, this locomotive is currently (November 2005)
undergoing overhaul at Stewarts Lane and is expected to return to the main line
early in 2006.

*Right:* Busy times at Brockenhurst on 27 August 1966. Apparently ignored by
the crew resting on the platform, No 35014 *Nederland Line* runs through on its
way to Southampton with the 11.30 Bournemouth–Waterloo. On the left are the
engine and stock for the Lymington-branch service, whilst the goods yard
beyond is well stocked with vehicles.

*Left:* With hand-signalling in operation, No 35016 *Elder Fyffes* emerges from Southampton Tunnel and coasts into Southampton Central station with the down 'Belle' on 5 September 1964. Eastleigh men recall this machine as being average amongst the class — predictable but uninspiring would be another way of describing it — although much depended on the willingness or otherwise of the men in charge.

*Above:* No 35025 *Brocklebank Line* presents a delightful sight as it speeds south through Micheldever with the down 'Belle' on 12 October 1963. In the background can be seen evidence of the deep chalk excavations carried out at the turn of the century, when spoil from here was used in connection with the LSWR's dock expansion at Southampton, which afforded space for a considerable number of storage sidings at this location.

*Above:* No 35005 *Canadian Pacific*, the only one of the first 10 engines of its type to be built that did not exceed one million miles in revenue-earning service. It is seen just south of Swaythling in charge of a rake of what appears to be predominantly Maunsell stock, heading for St Denys and Southampton on 24 March 1961.

*Right:* During what was destined to be its last full year of operation, No 35015 *Rotterdam Lloyd* passes St Denys signalbox with a down working on 12 April 1963. Despite having received a light casual overhaul in December 1962/January 1963 the engine was recorded as 'stored unserviceable' on 6 January 1964 and thus had the sorry distinction of being the first of the class to be deemed as such. Along with No 35002 it was officially withdrawn in February 1964.

*Above left:* Happier times for No 35014 *Nederland Line*, passing the sign for Brockenhurst Manor Golf Club with the down 'Bournemouth Belle'. On the right is Lymington Junction signalbox, controlling the divergence of three routes — the branch to Lymington, the main line to Sway, and the 'old road' via Ringwood.

*Left:* A personal favourite with the author was No 35012 *United States Lines* seen here in apparently first-rate condition with an up Waterloo train just north of Allbrook on 23 May 1962. Appropriately this engine was also used to later haul Gresley 'A4' No 60008 *Dwight D. Eisenhower* to Eastleigh *en route* to Southampton Docks and ultimately preservation in the USA. Sadly No 35012 would not be so lucky and was withdrawn in April 1967 due to severe difficulties with the regulator. This failing was so bad that steam would leak past the regulator valve to such an extent that, even with the valve supposed fully shut, steam was still reaching the valves and pistons. BR had received a request

from the American delegation that No 35012 should one day join the 'A4', but this was not to be, and No 35012 was turned into a pile of unidentifiable scrap.

*Above:* No 35018 *British India Line* passes Henstridge with an RCTS special on 6 March 1966 — the only occasion on which a 'Merchant Navy' worked over the Somerset & Dorset line. The type was officially banned due to weight restrictions, but, as was reported in contemporary magazines, at this late stage in the life of the S&D such considerations no longer seemed to matter. This particular locomotive lasted in service until August 1964 before being sold to Woodham Bros at Barry, where it languished until sold for preservation in 1980. Ironically the fact that No 35018 was one of the early casualties probably meant that it was in better condition than some which survived until the very end, although cannibalisation allied to years of exposure to salt spray at Barry meant that when it was eventually purchased it was little more than a rusty shell. One day, perhaps, No 35018 will steam again.

*Above:* Another single-line working, this time at Itchen Abbas on the now closed section of the Mid-Hants line south of Alresford. No 35008 is seen in charge of a diverted Bournemouth service on 1 May 1966, at which time electrification work meant that a number of steam services were routed this way, particularly at weekends. Despite the filth the engine displays no obvious steam leaks and (as recounted earlier) would survive to the end of SR steam.

*Right:* Our final view of a 'Merchant Navy' features No 35023 *Holland Afrika Line* leaving Bournemouth Central with the 12.25pm down relief service to Weymouth on 10 June 1967. (Remember the days when the operators would put on a relief train if passenger numbers demanded it …? With just one month to go the locomotive still appears in 'reasonable nick', as was confirmed by an Eastleigh driver who recalled the violent bout of slipping he had experienced a couple of years earlier at Hook with sister engine No 35004 *Cunard White Star*.

*Above:* We now turn our attention to Bulleid's Light Pacific type, although to the untrained eye there was little to distinguish this from the heavier 'Merchant Navy'. Indeed, remove name- and numberplates and it would take a skilful observer to determine the difference! This is 'West Country' No 34106 *Lydford*, in poor condition externally but apparently working well as it passes Tisbury with an up West of England working on 29 August 1964. The following month, however, and for reasons that are not reported, No 34106 was laid aside, never to work again; possibly it was simply in need of an overhaul, which by then would not have been authorised, or maybe it was a victim of the regular inside-cylinder or frame problems that beset so many of the class. The actual reason is unlikely ever to be known, for the locomotive was sold for scrap and cut up at Swansea before the year was out.

*Above right:* A Light Pacific in basically original form, prior to being rebuilt. 'Battle of Britain' No 34050 *Royal Observer Corps* is seen on 13 October 1956 at Southampton Central, where, judging from its position alongside Platform 5, it was acting as the down pilot. At the time just 10 years old, it would survive in this form for a further two years. The original side raves on the tender make an interesting comparison with the cut-down versions seen in the preceding and following photographs.

*Right:* No 34079 *141 Squadron* ex works at Eastleigh in August 1959, having reportedly just received its AWS (Automatic Warning System) equipment as well as having its tender modified as shown. AWS was a welcome safety feature, although ironically not all of the South Western Division main lines were fully equipped, whilst (it was said) the system was not totally reliable in the London area due to interference from the third rail. For some time based at Exmouth Junction, this locomotive would return to that shed following a satisfactory period of running in on local turns from Eastleigh.

*Above:* A summer holiday in 1962 allowed Tony the opportunity to record trains at (to him) unfamiliar locations but hauled in many cases by locomotives seen on a regular basis in his native Hampshire. Here we see a 'West Country' actually in the West Country, as a somewhat begrimed No 34030 *Watersmeet* passes the limited locomotive facilities at Ilfracombe with the 10.30am Ilfracombe–Exeter passenger service on 3 August 1962. One of a number of locomotives transferred to Western Region control following a revision of boundaries at the end of 1962, No 34030 was destined to survive until September 1964.

*Right:* No 34060 *25 Squadron* at Exeter St Davids — Western Region territory — on 16 July 1960, during its last few months in original condition. Following its arrival from the West Country the train will form the 10.20am to Waterloo via Exeter Central and Salisbury; Exeter St Davids was one of the few locations in the country where, due to 19th-century railway history, trains for London could leave in either direction, depending upon the route being taken. In October, following completion of the summer service, the locomotive was taken into works at Eastleigh, emerging at the end of the following month in rebuilt form and also with AWS and a speedometer fitted.

A classic view taken this time in North Devon, featuring No 34070 *Manston* at Barnstaple with the 1.32pm Exeter train, again from Ilfracombe, on 31 July 1962. As was usual, the train consists of only a few vehicles, the locomotives' gluttonous appetite for coal doing little to keep down costs on what was generally a poorly patronised part of the railway system.

Another view on the SR's 'Withered Arm', again at Barnstaple, on 31 July 1962, this time featuring a down train. No 34023 has just left the town ready for its run through Wrafton, Braunton and Morthoe to its destination at Ilfracombe.

Just visible on the extreme right is an Ivatt Class 2 2-6-2T working what is probably a Torrington-bound service.

*Above:* A grey day in March 1961 finds No 34041 *Wilton* working the 2.15pm Bournemouth West–Waterloo train near Swaythling. This locomotive was withdrawn — from Eastleigh shed — in January 1966, simply because it had become due for works attention.

*Right:* No 34023 *Blackmore Vale* hard at work on the main line near Semley with the Plymouth–Brighton through train on 29 August 1964. This was one of just two unrebuilt locomotives to last to the very end, the other being No 34102 *Lapford*. Restored to its original malachite green as SR No 21C123, *Blackmore Vale* now has a secure home in preservation on the Bluebell Railway in East Sussex, but No 34102 was not so fortunate, being scrapped at Newport in September 1968.

*Above:* Returning now to Hampshire, we see the down 'Pines Express', complete with its usual rake of standard BR Mk 1 maroon coaches, passing Worting Junction, west of Basingstoke, behind No 34084 *253 Squadron* in the late afternoon of 12 October 1963. In later years this service was regularly hauled by No 34102 *Lapford*.

*Right:* Light work for No 34080 *74 Squadron* near Tisbury on 29 August 1964. By now based at Exmouth Junction, the locomotive displays evidence of previous hard work — notice the burnt paintwork on the smokebox. However, this may have indicated a mechanical problem, for withdrawal came just a week or so later.

*Left:* Alongside one of the Western Region DMUs employed on Bristol–Portsmouth trains, No 34066 *Spitfire*, complete with white-painted smokebox-door hinges, pauses at Southampton Central while working an up Waterloo service on 11 April 1966. This particular embellishment appeared on several engines around this time but with hindsight did little but accentuate an often run-down appearance. No 34066 was well regarded by Salisbury crews, but its general condition led to its withdrawal from that shed six months after the photograph was taken.

*Above:* No 34105 *Swanage* near Radley with the down 'Pines Express' on 9 May 1964. The same locomotive had earlier in the day hauled the up working, which due to a derailment at Reading West had to be diverted via the DNS line through Newbury. The passengers that morning had the dubious distinction of being the last fare-paying passengers to travel the DNS route through to Newbury before final closure just a few months later.

On more local territory No 34038 *Lynton* edges slowly into the old Eastern Docks at Southampton with the 'Venus' boat train on 16 September 1961. Then based at Eastleigh, No 34038 was for some time a regular performer on Southampton–Reading parcels trains and when the photograph was taken had only recently emerged from what was destined to be its last general overhaul. For many years the Light Pacifics were the favoured locomotives for the boat trains, the reasoning being that it did not do to send 'rival' motive power to the ships being met!

As might be expected the Bulleid Pacifics were used on a number of steam specials, particularly in the latter years. Sunday 3 July 1966 saw No 34002 *Salisbury* working the last leg of an LCGB railtour from Waterloo, which had travelled west as far as Yeovil, before turning south to Weymouth and returning via Bournemouth, where the 'West Country' took over. The train is seen bathed in evening sunshine at Stoneham, just south of Eastleigh.

*Above:* A beautifully turned out 'West Country', No 34020 *Seaton*, running through the New Forest with what, according to the headcode, purports to be a Waterloo service but which, judging from the coaching stock, could well be an inter-regional working. The date was 23 April 1962, at which time the locomotive was allocated to Exmouth Junction and had not (according to records) had a recent works visit, making its presence on the Bournemouth line somewhat puzzling.

*Right:* Broadstone in 1966, and the combination of 'U'-class 2-6-0 No 31639 and 'West Country' Pacific No 34015 *Exmouth*. The date is 1 January, and the pair are waiting to depart with an RCTS special to Bath Green Park, 'Merchant

Navy' No 35011 having brought the train hither from Waterloo. No 34015 appears in excellent external condition and would even receive a light casual repair as late as April/May 1966. In view of the (accurate) comments made earlier about the prohibition of steam repairs after 1964 this might appear somewhat strange, but by now it was known by the traffic operators at Waterloo that if they wanted steam to continue until electrification completed then they had to effect some heavier maintenance than was achievable in the course of day-to-day work at the sheds. No 34015 was thus one of the last to benefit, but this was only putting off the inevitable, and when further repairs became necessary the engine was withdrawn in April 1967.

*Above:* The regular 'Pines Express' engine after 1964 was No 34102 *Lapford*, seen here just south of Winchester Junction with the down service on 16 October 1964. This was another locomotive destined to receive works repairs very late in life, enabling it to survive until the very end of Southern steam but, sadly, not into preservation, No 34102 being reduced to scrap at Newport, South Wales, in the summer of 1968.

*Above right:* No 34067 *Tangmere*, one of four of the class named after World War 2 fighter stations on the South Coast. RAF Tangmere was located just east of Chichester, although the locomotive of the same name was recorded on 19 June 1961 north of Allbrook (Eastleigh) with the 5.20pm Waterloo–Bournemouth semi-fast.

*Right:* Serviced and awaiting its next tour of duty at Eastleigh MPD on 11 May 1963, No 34038 *Lynton* reposes next to another longtime Eastleigh engine, Ivatt Class 2 Mogul No 41319. The 'West Country' had yet to make its final works visit (at the end of 1963), which would prolong its life until mid-1966.

*Above left:* A sight impossible to recapture today, and not merely because this particular locomotive no longer survives. No 34102 *Lapford*, unusually (for the period) still in possession its original nameplates, coasts along light-engine south of Shawford in April 1967. Since that time a failure to cut back foliage beside the track in this area has meant there is little for either the passenger ('customer'?) or the lineside observer to see at this point. The cleanliness of the locomotive suggests recent or anticipated special-train working, but this cannot be confirmed.

*Left:* Double-heading of any sort on the South Western main line was unusual, especially this kind of super-power. Nos 34023 and 34108, formerly named

*Blackmore Vale* and *Wincanton* respectively, are seen in charge of an RCTS special, bound for Salisbury between Eastleigh and Romsey on 18 June 1967.

*Above:* Performing well on the climb north of Winchester, No 34086 *219 Squadron* has charge of what is obviously the up 'Bournemouth Belle' on 30 August 1964. It was very unusual not to find one of the larger 'Merchant Navy' locomotives on this working, and No 34086 appears none too clean either, albeit mechanically sound, there being no obvious steam leaks. The leading vehicle is a BR Full Brake in chocolate and cream, one of the pair transferred from the Western Region, to augement the stowage space when required.

*Left:* Stopping-train duty for No 34093 *Saunton* at Hook, east of Basingstoke, in April 1962 at the head of the 12.54pm Waterloo service. By this time this working was more usually the province of BR Standard locomotives than the former SR types.

*Above:* No 34052 *Lord Dowding* gets away from Salisbury with the 7.39pm to Waterloo on 4 July 1964. In the bay (left) is one of the 'Hampshire' DEMU units, which had probably arrived from Southampton via Romsey.

*Above:* Captured from the station footbridge on 29 May 1965, No 34087 *145 Squadron*, by now an Eastleigh-based locomotive, disturbs the peace at an otherwise deserted Swaythling station with a down through passenger working. This locomotive was a particular favourite with a number of Eastleigh crews, their allegiance having altered over the years from the days when Bulleids were rarely seen at Eastleigh in favour of the Maunsell 'Lord Nelson' 4-6-0. By 1965 the 'Nelsons' were but a memory, and No 34087 seems well in charge of the 12.35 Waterloo–Bournemouth passenger service.

*Right, top to bottom:* Amongst Tony's photographic records are a number of nameplate views, usually recorded when the locomotive was newly ex works from Eastleigh and either on a running-in turn or awaiting return to its home shed. On 6 June 1963 it was the nameplate of No 34010 that was 'snapped',

whilst another photograph taken on 8 September 1961 recorded that of sister locomotive No 34017. Another, undated record featured the plate belonging to No 34028, which, being named after the Eddystone Rock, had no civic crest. Finally the plate from No 34040 was photographed as late as 7 May 1966, when the locomotive was awaiting what would be its final works overhaul, carried out between 13 May and 10 June 1966.

*Far right, top to bottom:* Having featured the nameplates of a selection of 'West Country' Pacifics, we turn now to the 'Battle of Britain' locomotives, with examples from Nos 34076, 34088 and 34109. That from No 34076 is on an unrebuilt engine, whilst *Sir Trafford Leigh Mallory* was one of the longer plates, although not the largest, that distinction being held by No 34090 *Sir Eustace Missenden — Southern Railway.*

SIDMOUTH

WEST COUNTRY CLASS

ILFRACOMBE

WEST COUNTRY CLASS

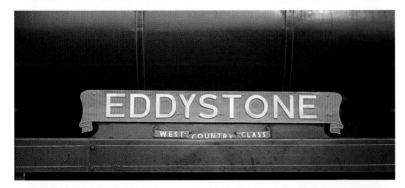

EDDYSTONE

WEST COUNTRY CLASS

CREWKERNE

WEST COUNTRY CLASS

41 SQUADRON

BATTLE OF BRITAIN CLASS

SEEK AND DESTROY

IRRITATUS LACESSIT CRABRO

213 SQUADRON

BATTLE OF BRITAIN CLASS

SIR TRAFFORD LEIGH MALLORY

BATTLE OF BRITAIN CLASS

*Above:* Rebuilt 'West Country' No 34010 *Sidmouth* outside the front of Eastleigh shed on 6 June 1963, shortly after emerging from the neighbouring works following what was to be its final works visit. The evening sun has highlighted a patch on the lower part of the tender, which area was prone to leakage due to flexing and corrosion of the (very thin) side plates.

*Left:* No 34095 *Brentor* appears well in charge of its train as it speeds through Micheldever with the 10.30am Waterloo–Bournemouth service on 12 August 1961. The locomotive had emerged from rebuilding only seven months previously and was thus in peak condition.

One of the final steam-hauled boat trains to enter Southampton Docks in the summer of 1967. 'West Country' No 34018 *Axminster*, based at Nine Elms for the last few months of its life, is seen cautiously threading its way towards the Ocean Terminal with a mixed rake of green and BR blue/grey stock. Both driver and fireman are leaning out of the left side of the cab and so cannot see the flagman on the opposite side of the track.

*Above:* Another boat train, this time a down Channel Islands working destined for Weymouth on 12 September 1965 and recorded between Shawford Junction and Shawford station. The locomotive is No 34104 *Bere Alston*.

*Right:* Rebuilt examples of both series are seen together at Totton on 18 June 1967 with the Southampton–Wareham leg of an RCTS special from Waterloo. The locomotives involved were 'West Country' No 34108 (formerly *Wincanton*) and 'Battle of Britain' No 34089 (*602 Squadron*), both having had their nameplates removed as was customary at this late stage to thwart souvenir-hunters.

*Above left:* A smart rake of green-liveried BR Mk 1 coaches (complete with Southern Region formation number) make up the through Bournemouth–York train, seen here at Hinton Admiral, in the New Forest, on 22 April 1962. The engine is No 34009 *Lyme Regis*, not as yet AWS-fitted, which modification was supposedly carried out in 1960/1 at the same time as the engine was rebuilt in the form shown; the absence of an AWS battery box gives credence to the suggestion that contemporary works records of modifications may not always be 100% accurate. The scorching on the smokebox door is evidence of previous hard work.

*Left:* An interesting line-up of coaching stock behind No 34037 *Clovelly* near Micheldever on 12 August 1961. The train is the 8.35 Bournemouth West–Waterloo, which appears to consist of a three-coach Maunsell set, a single BR Mk 1 vehicle still in 'blood and custard' and a six-coach Bulleid restaurant-car set.

*Above:* Another mixed rake consisting of a BR Mk 1 — this time in green — sandwiched between Bulleid coaches. No 34017 *Ilfracombe* has steam to spare as it coasts down the bank between Winchester Junction and Winchester with a Bournemouth-bound service on 9 September 1961. Just two weeks later the locomotive would be admitted to Eastleigh Works for overhaul, having run for four years since rebuilding in 1957.

Maroon stock was seen on the Southern Region just two or three times a day, being used on the various inter-regional services. On 9 June 1962 12 coaches were required for the Bournemouth–Wolverhampton through train, seen in Shawford Cutting behind No 34039 *Boscastle*. Usually the SR locomotive would take the train as far as Oxford, returning either with a return passenger working or occassionally with a freight, via Newbury.

Another view of No 34050 *Royal Observer Corps* (see page 29), this time on 15 May 1964 in rebuilt form and easily identifiable by the coloured badges below the number on the cabside. The location is between Allbrook and Eastleigh on the down through line, the service a boat train for Southampton Docks. In the background the Allbrook starting signals are in the 'off' position for up trains on both through and relief lines.

*Above:* As stated previously, it was unusual to see any of the Bulleid Pacific classes on freight, although their use on such workings was not unknown. Towards the end of steam almost anything went, and on 15 June 1967 No 34087, formerly named *145 Squadron*, was rostered by the Eastleigh list clerk for what appears to be a mixed working, possibly bound for Eastleigh yard and photographed near what would later be Southampton Airport/Parkway station. In the background is the Ford complex at Swaythling well-known as the 'Home of the Transit'. Today the M27 motorway crosses the railway by way of an overbridge at almost exactly this point.

*Right:* Spruced to perfection, No 34089 *602 Squadron* has charge of just four vehicles forming the Royal Train as it passes Allbrook on the down through line on 5 August 1961; regrettably the identity of the VIP on board has not been established. Notice the burnished coupling and buffers, all of which were specially fitted for the occasion and would be removed and replaced by everyday gear after the duty.

*Left:* A rarely photographed angle of a rebuilt 'West Country' — notice where the cleaners have (and, more interestingly, have not) been able to reach. The location, on the main line west of Salisbury, is Dinton station, which No 34005 *Barnstaple* is about to leave with the 4.10pm stopping service to Waterloo on 29 August 1964. This locomotive had been the first of the Light Pacifics to be rebuilt in the form shown, emerging thus in May 1957.

*Above:* Easy work for No 34004 *Yeovil* on the 3.10pm down stopping service near Hinton Admiral on 23 April 1962. This locomotive was for many years one of the most regular performers on the Bournemouth line, being based at Bournemouth and Eastleigh during its life.

*Above left:* Another regular protagonist on the Bournemouth line was No 34093 *Saunton*, rebuilt in May 1960 and depicted here just south of Shawford a year later, on 13 May 1961. The train is the 12.35pm Waterloo–Weymouth, running 'main line' towards Allbrook and Eastleigh.

*Left:* No 34089 *602 Squadron*, recorded shortly after its Royal Train duty (see page 61) and still in superb external condition at Eastleigh in August 1961. It is a pity that the care lavished externally could not have been extended to the

simple expedient of closing the lid to the tender tank, whilst the coal on top of the cab, if not cleared off manually, will very shortly fall off by itself.

*Above:* Sister locomotive No 34087 *145 Squadron* with the down 'Iberia' boat train at Micheldever on 2 September 1961. The scheduling of boat trains in the down direction was simple enough, but the vagaries of the Atlantic weather made up services much less predictable.

Another down boat train, this time on 14 June 1967 and more easily identified, thanks to the 'Holland–America' headboard. The engine is believed to be No 34013 *Okehampton*, all boat trains by now being in the hands of Eastleigh men and machines. The location is just south of Eastleigh, alongside what was still primarily the grass of Southampton/Eastleigh airport. This, incidentally, had only recently installed its first concrete runway, at the end of which was placed a barrel of beer for the men, in recognition of their work.

Concluding for the moment our look at steam-hauled boat trains on the South Western, No 34009 *Lyme Regis* is seen shunting its train in Southampton New (Western) Docks on 26 April 1964. The shunter riding on the footstep will be noted.

*Left:* Although at the time officially based at Salisbury, No 34032 *Camelford* heads a down service through the New Forest on 23 April 1962; had it been 'borrowed' to cover a failure? The location, on the Bournemouth direct line through Sway, is easily identifiable from the twin bridges on this section, which differed in design from those elsewhere. This was one of the stretches of line where the Bulleid locomotives were at greatest risk of setting light to adjoining land, and it was primarily to reduce the emission of sparks and cinders (rather than to improve steaming, which came as a bonus) that sister locomotive No 34064 was fitted with a Giesl ejector. Indeed, the end of steam brought relief to staff working in the Southern Region's legal offices, for no longer would they be inundated with claims from farmers for crop damage, which was easy to allege and difficult to disprove.

*Above:* Framed by the Andover Road overbridge just north of Winchester City station on 7 August 1965, No 34044 *Woolacombe* slows for the stop with a relief to the down 'Pines'. The fact this is the relief train explains the mixed maroon and green rake, the first coach of which appears to be an ex-LMS vehicle, unusually with maroon-painted ends. The locomotive is in generally poor external condition, whilst the presence of conductor-rail (in the 'four-foot' of the up main) waiting to be laid bodes ill for the future of steam on the route.

*Above:* No 34017 *Ilfracombe* approaches Wallers Ash, north of Winchester, with a Waterloo-bound service on 16 June 1962. At this time it was still the practice to ensure that the banks alongside the track were kept clear of vegetation, which not only reduced the fire risk but also made signal-sighting easier from greater distances.

*Right:* On 7 July 1967, just two days before the end of Southern steam, No 34021, formerly named *Dartmoor*, arrives at Eastleigh off the Portsmouth line with empty coaching stock. The impending demise of steam aside, the railway had already seen many changes in terms of infrastructure, the yard in the background being almost empty of traffic, whilst the colour-light signals have removed the need for the heavy gantry, which will shortly be removed for scrap.

Two days later on 9 July 1967 came No 34021's very last working, on the final day of operational steam on the Southern Region. Seen between Swaythling and Southampton/Eastleigh Airport, this was also the final steam-hauled boat train from Southampton, the vessel served understood to have been the Greek Line's *Ellinis*.

On that fateful Sunday afternoon Eastleigh presented a melancholy appearance. At the rear of the shed, where once there would have been a hive of activity as locomotives were prepared early for the next day's duty, now stands a single line of redundant motive power awaiting removal; nearest the camera is rebuilt 'Battle of Britain' No 34077, withdrawn some four months earlier. By midnight the shed roads would be empty. Although the sidings remain today for use by more modern traction, the shed building and steam facilities were removed with almost indecent haste.

*Left:* Towards the end of steam on the Southern coaching stock became more of a mix and match than before; as can be seen within these pages blue/grey-liveried coaches were to be seen. Here No 34108 *Wincanton* works an up Waterloo train, comprising of BR and Bulleid-designed green-liveried stock, near Brockenhurst on 27 August 1966.

*Right:* For many years a very rare visitor to the South Western area, having been based originally on the South Eastern section, rebuilt 'West Country' No 34100 *Appledore* awaits its next duty at Eastleigh on 11 May 1963. By the date the '700' class 0-6-0 had already been withdrawn.

*Below right:* When originally rebuilt the Southern Region saw steam continuing until 1975. With this in mind No 34039 *Boscastle* is seen ex works in the winter sunshine at Eastleigh in January 1960. No 34039 has just emerged after rebuilding and unusually with the background to the nameplate painted black; were any others of the class treated the same way?

The fact that the Southern Region possessed some 140 Pacifics — more than twice as many as the LMR — meant that 'intrusions' by 4-6-2 types from other regions were not that common. Indeed, for a brief period in the early 1960s all 140 Bulleids were concentrated on the South Western Division, making it possible to observe them even on short trains, as there were more than enough to go around. This led to the withdrawal of older designs — the Maunsell 'Nelson' and 'Schools' classes, for example — after which it was the Bulleid breed that dominated the scene for the remaining years of steam operation.

However, as time passed and steam nationwide was relegated to lesser duties, Pacifics appeared from elsewhere, either on ordinary or (later) on special workings; previously it would have been difficult to spare top-link machines in this way. Accordingly on 17 August 1966 'Britannia' No 70004, formerly *William Shakespeare* and itself once the pride of Stewarts Lane, is seen at Eastleigh on more menial duties with a banana train from Southampton Docks *en route* back to its latter-day home in the Midlands.

Another 'Britannia', but this time capturing the attention of a number of enthusiasts. No 70020 *Mercury* is seen on 8 March 1964 at Ludgershall, then the southern stump of the former MSWJ route, with an enthusiasts' special — the 'South Western Rambler' — organised by the Southern Counties Touring Society. No 70020 was utilised on the initial leg from Waterloo via Ascot and Reading to Salisbury, including the Ludgershall trip, after which '9F' 2-10-0 No 92209 took over between Salisbury, Templecombe and Bournemouth, No 70020 in the meantime having made its way from Salisbury to Bournemouth for the final leg back to Waterloo.

Reference has earlier (page 24) been made to the presence of a Gresley 'A4' Pacific at Eastleigh, when No 60008 *Dwight D. Eisenhower* was stabled temporarily at the Hampshire shed on its way to Southampton Docks and preservation in the USA. On that occasion (illustrated in our earlier book *The Heyday of Eastleigh and its Locomotives*) the 'A4' was 'dead', but such was not the case on 16 March 1963, when No 60022 *Mallard* was recorded heading light-engine for Eastleigh shed in readiness for a special working the following day.

Another ex-LNER Pacific, the (by now) privately preserved Gresley 'A3'
No 4472 *Flying Scotsman*, undergoes servicing at Eastleigh on 18 May 1963
prior to returning north later the same day with a special from Southampton to
Banbury, Derby and Worksop.

A final view of a Southern Region steam special organised by the RCTS. Starting from Waterloo, this particular tour, on 18 June 1967, took in Guildford, Fareham, Southampton, Swanage, Weymouth, Eastleigh and Salisbury before returning to Waterloo. The Fareham–Southampton leg was entrusted to No 34089, seen here at Mount Pleasant on what was clearly a cloudless summer's afternoon.